I0176914

Free Indeed

Palmetto
PUBLISHING GROUP

WWW.PALMETTOPUBLISHINGGROUP.COM

Palmetto Publishing Group, LLC
Charleston, SC

For information on regarding special discounts for bulk
purchases, please contact Palmetto Publishing Group at
Info@PalmettoPublishingGroup.com

ISBN-13: 978-1-944313-01-2
ISBN-10: 194431301X

Free Indeed

Veronica Smith

Table of Contents

Acknowledgements

First and foremost, I would like to thank my Lord and Savior Jesus Christ for loving me in spite of myself, for showering me with His grace and mercy, and for never leaving me, especially during the times when I felt the loneliest. A very heartfelt thank you to my husband Starklen for supporting and encouraging me throughout this process. For their unwavering love, and for allowing me the quiet time I needed to pour my story out on paper, I'd like to thank my children, Chesney, Amari, Phillip, and Jaylen. A colossal thank you to Arestina for allowing God to use you to help me to see that it is well. Aletta P., as usual, you were the coach/organizer I needed at the beginning of the process. You helped me bring the thoughts in my head into focus and organize what already made sense to me so it would make sense for everyone else. I can't thank you enough. To my study groups, thank you so much for your participation. Your suggestions were very helpful and greatly appreciated. I love you all.

Thank you Palmetto Publishing Group (Michael, Jen, and everyone else who I did not have the pleasure of meeting). Thank you for your guidance, patience, and professionalism. I don't know how I would have gotten any of this completed had it not been for you. Katrina (editor), thank you for your keen eye. You helped me to polish my story and make it shine.

Foreword

Put to death, therefore, whatever belongs to your earthly nature: sexual immorality, impurity, lust, evil desires and greed, which is idolatry (Col. 3:5).

I'm writing these words to serve as a warning to everyone, but especially to women who feel they can watch pornography without it affecting them. I want everyone to be aware of the lure of the spirit of pornography and how it can sneak up on you and become an addiction before you even realize it's happening. It can begin with something we think is harmless, like a romance novel, and cause you to end up in a place you never thought you'd be. A place that's lonely and full of guilt, shame, and condemnation. That's exactly where I ended up–until I fully accepted the freedom that was already mine. Take these words to heart and learn from them.

Pay attention to your children. Keep tabs on the things they're searching on their mobile devices. With the clicks of just a few buttons, graphic, pornographic images could pop up on the screen and cause them to begin their own journey to imprisonment. Be careful of with whom you allow them to have sleepovers. There could be a trap in their friend's home that was not meant to be a trap for children, but it could end up changing your child's whole life. Purge your homes of anything even remotely resembling pornography.

I was just nine years old when I was introduced to the world of pornography through an article in an erotic magazine. There were no pictures, just words, but I knew from the moment I began reading that I had to see what those words described.

While trying to decide if I was going to be obedient to the Lord and tell my story, I began to ask my loved ones and others around me about the questions they would ask a female who was addicted to pornography. Some of the responses I received were frightening. They were questions I never wanted to have to answer. I had hidden these secrets for years and didn't want anyone to ever find out about them. I didn't want people to see me as anything other than the quiet, sweet "good girl" they thought I was. However, freedom comes with honesty, and to be free indeed meant that I had to be honest. I am aware that some of you will find my truth hard to receive, especially coming from a female, but for those who need it, I pray that you are able to find your freedom through my testimony.

Some of the events throughout the following sections may seem to repeat themselves. They happened simultaneously, but I separated them and tried to tell them in different ways to ensure that I answered the questions fully and honestly.

So, this is my journey.

Create in me a clean heart, O God; and renew a right spirit within me (Ps. 51:10).

Section 1

The Story

How was your childhood/family life? How did events from your past and the choices you made contribute to your addiction?

Enter through the narrow gate. For wide is the gate and broad is the road that leads to destruction, and many enter through it. But small is the gate and narrow the road that leads to life, and only a few find it (Matt. 7:13-14).

My parents had six children. We lived in a four-bedroom home with one bathroom. Both of my parents worked until my father became ill and had to have a kidney transplant. There wasn't always a lot of money, but we had everything we needed.

They took us to church every Sunday. They taught us morals and values and how to behave, whether we were in their presence or not. So, what I did went against everything I knew was right. However, we weren't a family that laid issues out and discussed them. When things happened, they just happened. We "got over it" and moved on. We never really got over anything, though, because nothing was ever really dealt with, just buried. We all know what happens when we try to bury something that's still alive. We had to live with those zombies. They just kept coming back.

On top of not understanding the importance of discussing issues, I was an introverted child with low self-esteem, so any time I experienced anything troublesome, no one knew. I kept it to myself. That's how my life went: I kept everything to myself. No one knew that I'd found erotic reading material in the house, and I certainly wasn't going to tell them. The more curious I became, the more I searched for erotic books. The more I searched, the more I found. I remember reading that first essay and wondering why my body started to feel different. It was a strange, new, and wonderful sensation that I liked very much. So I kept reading. That was the beginning of the bondage that would keep me captive for years. I had opened myself up for the spirit of pornography to enter my life, but that spirit didn't come alone. It brought its friends—lust, fear, doubt, guilt, shame, distraction, and condemnation—with it. They took turns and worked overtime, trying to keep me from my destiny. Soon, reading wasn't enough.

Reading those impure words turned into a desire to see those things I read about. I couldn't get the fix I needed from just reading anymore. My quiet, laid-back, shy personality actually made it easy for me to sneakily watch the one video I'd been able to find. The fact that I could sneak and do this actually became my driving force. I could do this because no one suspected the "good girl" of any wrongdoing. I was playing a dangerous game that

Create in me a clean heart, O God; and renew a right spirit within me (Ps. 51:10).

quickly became serious, and before I realized it, I was trapped. I had to have it.

Growing up, I never felt like I fit in. I had friends but felt they were all better than me. Their families had more money, their cars were newer, they were smarter, and they wore trendier clothes. The shallow thoughts of a child. I never told any of them that I felt this way; I was shy and timid, and wouldn't speak up for myself. Sometimes I allowed my friends to make decisions for me. Things were said and done to me, and I just "got over it." That's how I coped with life. I "got over it."

I remember a junior high school teacher saying something mean to me, and the whole class laughing. He didn't know that he had added fuel to the self-doubt smoldering in me. I felt so dumb. I grew up in a small town where there was only one elementary, one junior high, and one high school. My peers and I saw each other all the time. I had to live with feeling insignificant and small—and some classmates often reminded me (sometimes knowingly, sometimes unknowingly) of it until I left for college.

My outlet became pornography. I could forget the real, cruel world for a while and live in the fantasy. I lived vicariously through the fake emotions that the actors displayed. They filled each other's desires, and I wanted what they appeared to be giving each other. My strongest yearning was to feel wanted. I know now that I was wanted, but back then, I didn't feel that way.

I am grateful, however, that all those images in my head and my need to feel wanted didn't cause me to become promiscuous. My personality and the persistent fear that followed me wouldn't allow it. I'm not saying that I was innocent. Things happened, things that made me physically ill and disgusted with myself, and I vowed to leave the stunts up to the professionals. I thank God because had I acted on some of the thoughts I had, this story would be very different. Thank you, Jesus. It wasn't what it could have been.

It wasn't until my sophomore year of college that I began to believe in *me*. One day, doubt was really working on me. I knew I wanted to teach, but because of what had been said to me in junior high school and the taunts I'd received as a result, I doubted that I had the ability to teach. After all, what child would benefit from being taught by a dummy like me?

On this particular day, my sophomore advisor looked at me and said, "You're a born teacher." I was surprised that she could see what hadn't been spoken: all of the self-doubt. Until that point in my life, I'd thought everyone viewed me in the same way. But Mrs. Connie Terry could see through the protective brick wall I'd built over the years to hide behind. She looked past the graffiti I had painted on that wall, constantly reminding myself that I was a dummy, I was fearful, I was an addict, and all the other nasty descriptors I had heard whispered in my direction over the years. She peered all the way down, to my purpose. Mrs. Terry's words shook me to my soul. Her words were like the kiss from Snow White's Prince Charming. She woke up the teacher that was lying dormant in me. She sparked a fire in me that still burns today. I can still hear her words and see her eyes piercing through my doubt and fear. "You're a born teacher." Thank you, Mrs. Terry, for speaking destiny into my life.

I love the teacher in me. When the teacher comes forth, everything else has to back her up. The teacher brings the Holy Spirit with her. She's confident and speaks with authority.

The problem with that was I couldn't teach twenty-four hours a day. So when I wasn't teaching, I allowed evil to once again slither its way into my mind. When I wasn't teaching or preparing to teach, my mind always reverted back to the thoughts that kept me in bondage.

Create in me a clean heart, O God; and renew a right spirit within me (Ps. 51:10).

Why do you think it was so hard to break away from your addiction?

You were taught, with regard to your former way of life, to put off your old self, which is being corrupted by its deceitful desires; to be made new in the attitude of your minds; and to put on the new self, created to be like God in true righteousness and holiness (Eph. 4:22-24).

Early on, my need for pornography transformed into a stress reliever and source of comfort (although lust always lurked in the background; I could feel its presence). I started using pornography as a solution. Anytime anything went wrong in my life (I called these moments breakdowns), I would tell myself, "I know what will make me feel better," and I would turn to porn. When I was caught up in that world, I felt comfortable. The actors in those videos were my friends, and I needed them. They were the only ones who understood how bad I felt about myself, and they were the only ones who knew how to make me feel better. They would put on a show for me whenever I needed one.

On bad days, the urges would get so strong. I would tell myself that I'd watch one scene, feel better, and be done. But it never happened that way. Once I opened that door, I was helpless to do anything but walk through it. I would binge for days at a time. Any free time I had was spent watching porn, reading porn, or thinking about porn. If I had a breakdown and didn't have access to my "friends," my mind would take me to them. That's when I started writing erotic poetry. During these intense breakdowns, I would cry and try to resist, but like a fisherman reeling in a big catch, it would lure me into its grip and release me only when I felt I could take no more. I would hear that nasty spirit whispering, *"Rest for a while, and we'll start again later."* Helplessly, I would do as I was told.

The shame that resulted from my addiction to pornography is what kept me in bondage for so long. I didn't want people to think poorly of me. After all, I was the "good girl." As a child, I didn't tell anyone because I was afraid they'd think I had bad parents. But they had no idea what I was doing. After I was married, I didn't talk about it because I certainly didn't want people to think I wasn't satisfied with my husband. And even he didn't know the full extent of my problem. My addiction had nothing to do with him. It began long before I knew him. Pornography had been a major part of my life since I was nine years old, and no one knew.

Even when I wanted to tell someone, I could hear the whispering hiss of condemnation: *"You're an addict. No one will want to be around you. They won't like you anymore. They'll talk about you and about your private struggle. Is it really worth the risk?"* This voice drained me of strength, and I was too weak to fight. So I kept my mouth shut. I kept all the anguish, torment, doubt, and fear to myself; and I suffered in silence.

Scenes from something I'd watched would pop into my head at the most inopportune moments. They'd invade my thoughts while I was trying to enjoy a movie with my family. We've watched some movies with certain scenes that are missing from my memory because I'd been caught up in my fantasy world. I didn't dare ask questions because I'd have to explain why I hadn't been paying attention when I'd been sitting there with everyone else. These thoughts would enter my mind when we went out to dinner. They'd pop up when we traveled. I remember being startled by my husband's voice one time because my mind had gone to my pornographic thoughts. I had forgotten that he was sitting right next to me in the car.

But most of the time, these thought would pop into my head when I did anything related to God. The spirit of distraction tried to keep me from developing a relationship with my God. Because I had not taken control over my own mind, the spirit of distraction assumed the responsibility. I allowed it to become the captain of my ship.

The spirit of distraction would whisper in my ear while I tried to study for Sunday school. It would whisper while I sat in Sunday school, listening to the teacher, and sometimes it tried while I was teaching Sunday school. The spirit of distraction never succeeded while I was teaching. Every nasty spirit trying to attack me would immediately back away when I taught. They all feared the teacher. They knew the teacher was sure and confident. Distraction would whisper in my ear when I led worship service in church. That's when I was the most tormented. I would sing and feel the presence of God, but at the same time hear I'd hear the whispering: *"God knows what you've been doing. He's disappointed and angry that you're standing before His people singing praises and pretending to love Him."* I would sing and cry. Sometimes I wouldn't be able to make it through a song because the whispering was so loud. During these times, I would stop singing and just cry.

My hands would sometimes still be lifted as I cried. To someone without a discerning spirit, it looked like I was caught up in a high praise. As soon as I'd throw the white flag of surrender and stop singing, I would hear the whispering turn into laughter. The spirit would trick me and then laugh when I fell for its tricks: a constant battle. People would approach me after service, telling me that the service was great, and that they loved how I'd been so caught up in the Lord that I couldn't finish a song. I would smile, thank them, and walk away quickly. Please don't get caught up in someone's talent. You need to be so in tune with the Lord that you can see through a beautiful voice and down to the possible torment inside, and then cry out in prayer for that tormented person. Sometimes someone would ask if everything was okay. They'd say that I had almost reached a breakthrough during praise, but then I had pulled it back in, like I'd been blocked by something (that fisherman again). I'd tell them that I was okay, but I could tell they knew I wasn't telling the truth. I also knew that they were praying for me.

I thank God for the prayers of those warriors. They helped me see that God never left me. Even when I allowed the whispering to overshadow Him, He was right there. As I sang praises to Him and as the spirits whispered in my ear, He was right there. He was with me all the time, waiting for me to realize that He would never forsake me, and that I had the power to fight. He was waiting for me to accept the freedom He'd been offering. He was so patient with me.

The Lord is not slack concerning His promise, as some men count slackness; but is longsuffering to us-ward, not willing that any should perish, but that all should come to repentance (2 Pet. 3:9).

Now when I cry, I'm crying because I'm filled with joy and a peace that passeth all understanding.

And the peace of God, which passeth all understanding, shall keep your hearts and minds through Christ Jesus (Phil. 4:7).

Create in me a clean heart, O God; and renew a right spirit within me (Ps. 51:10).

Worship leaders, we have an important job in the church. We stand before the congregation weekly, leading them into God's very presence. We should sing love songs to God, and our focus should only be on Him. If there is any hidden thing with the ability to take our focus off of God—possibly hindering others from finding Him—we need to make it right. We can't allow the devil to make us ashamed to confess our sins and be redeemed. God wants our best, and we can't give him our best if we're hoarding sinful secrets.

We need to open our mouths and tell someone (someone who is filled with and led by the Holy Spirit and is trustworthy, someone apt to teach you the truth of God's Word) so we can get the help we need. We don't have to stay imprisoned. We have not been given a life sentence. God *has* granted us a pardon.

As my mood changed, the type of porn I watched did as well. A slow, easy day was met with slow, easy porn. A long, frustrating, need-a-release kind of day was met with.... Well, you get the idea. I wouldn't need anything fixed on those slow and easy days, but lust would still rear its ugly head and whisper, *"You know you want it. It will make you feel good. We don't have to say a word. No one will ever know."* Sometimes I could fight lust off, and sometimes I couldn't. I felt more guilt and shame on the long and frustrating days than any other. On those days, it felt like the tears would never stop flowing. I would cry and pray as I was watched, telling God how sorry I was and showing Him that I knew what a disappointment I was. How could I be such a vile and disgusting person? I always felt worse after a porn binge than the day's frustrations had made me feel.

I never blamed God. I never asked why He wouldn't stop the enemy from picking on me; I already knew the answer. I had the power to stop them, but I was holding on. Mentally, I wasn't ready to rebuke the spirit of pornography. I was afraid to let go. We'd been together for so long that I didn't know how to live without it. If I let go, who would make me feel better when I was down? Who would stimulate me, even if I wasn't depressed?

God didn't create me that way. He gave me free will. I *learned* to use pornography to feel better. All I needed to do was accept His help, which He'd offered since the very beginning. He had been there the entire time, waiting for me to receive the healing that my mind, body, and soul so desperately needed and wanted.

I've always been hard on myself about everything, but when I'd have a breakdown, condemnation would take over, and the guilt would flood in. I'd ask myself, "How can you call yourself a Christian and still allow filth to pass through your eyes and consume your mind? How could God love you and want you on His team in the condition you're in?" I convinced myself that He had no use for me. It became a constant cycle of guilt, shame, depression, and remorse. What I was doing went against everything I believed and all I had been taught. Do you know how hard it was for me to be in that state of mind and keep it hidden from everyone? People told me that I always

Create in me a clean heart, O God; and renew a right spirit within me (Ps. 51:10).

looked happy. Some even said they'd never seen me without a smile on my face. I was an expert at pretending that everything was all right. I wish I could have opened myself up so they would have seen just how broken I was inside, and how much of a façade I had to put on every… single…day. No one knew, and no one understood how difficult it was for me to look different than I felt. It was physically and mentally exhausting, trying to constantly keep the mask on.

I only felt like my true self when I was caught up in porn. I didn't have to pretend with those people. I was comfortable with them. They knew exactly who I was, and I believed the lies. The person I was then was not the person God had created me to be. In the midst of my torment, people would come to me, seeking advice. It was amazing how easy it was for me to give others the advice, scriptures, and prayers they needed. It was hard for me to comprehend why God still chose to use me. In spite of what I was doing, in spite of the pretending, the guilt, the shame—in spite of myself, God still wanted to use me. He saw me as what He'd created me to be, and not who I thought I was. Before I was ever conceived, He knew the power I possessed through Him.

"Before I formed thee in the belly I knew thee; and before thou camest forth out of the womb I sanctified thee, *and* I ordained thee a prophet unto the nations" (Jer. 1:5).

Create in me a clean heart, O God; and renew a right spirit within me (Ps. 51:10).

When I think about it now, all I can say is, "Thank you, Jesus, for loving me when I didn't feel worthy of being loved." I understand now that helping others with their issues came so easily to me because, just like teaching, I was doing what I'd been created to do. I was allowing God to use me instead of falling prey to the enemy's tricks.

Was it hard trying to keep your children from finding out about the pornography and your addiction to it?

The wise woman builds her house, but with her own hands the foolish one tears hers down (Prov. 14:1).

One of the biggest fears I had during my addiction was that my children would find something inappropriate I'd hidden in the house—and end up trapped like I was. You would think that fear alone would have caused me to get rid of everything. I remember thinking how devastated I would be if one of my children ended up in bondage because I'd released that spirit into our home, but I couldn't stop. I needed it. It was my medicine.

So, how do you feed an addiction and keep your children from finding out about it? You guard it like Fort Knox. I didn't use the family computer to watch porn. I kept my own device just for that purpose, with the screen locked; and I kept it hidden from everyone. I definitely didn't sync it with the other devices in our house. I kept movies, books, and even the erotic poetry I'd written under lock and key; and I prayed to God that my family wouldn't find any of it.

This became more ammunition for the devil to use against me. *"You're not a mother, you're a perpetrator. What would your children think of you if they found out? They're going to hate you."* I believed it. I believed my children would be ashamed of me and would hate me if they found out, so I did everything in my power to keep that from happening. While my husband was at work, I would sit on my bed in front of the TV watching porn for hours, with a novel open on my lap, the remote in my hand, my finger on the power button. Anytime I'd hear anyone coming toward my bedroom, I would hit the power button, pick up the book, and pretend to have been reading. My family knew that I loved to read, so seeing me on my bed with the TV off and reading a book was normal. They didn't realize what was really going on. But the thought of them walking in before I could turn the TV off was too much for me to bear, so I started muting the TV to make sure I'd hear their footsteps. That didn't last long, though. The sounds were a part of the fantasy. It was like an alcoholic asking for a drink and being given a nonalcoholic one. There was something missing. Not being able to hear the sounds ruined it for me. I needed to not only see the fake enjoyment, but also to hear it to feel like I was being helped.

I felt like garbage inside. How could my children have respect for a mother like me? How could a mother behave this way with growing, impressionable children under the same roof? I should have been building my home by showing my children how to bask in God's presence, and to fear Him and follow His commandments, but instead I was slowly tearing it down brick by brick. I added each brick I'd removed from my home to the brick wall growing inside of me.

"Only be careful, and watch yourselves closely so that you do not forget the things your eyes have seen or let them fade from your heart as long as you live. Teach them to your children and to their children after them" (Deut. 4:9).

I had taken my focus off of the things of God. What could I teach my children? Could I say, "You should be honest at all times?" Could I say, "You can't hide from God, He sees everything?" Could I say, "Pornography is of the devil and you should never lay your eyes on it?" I did say all these things to my babies, and I continued to fall deeper into darkness. In essence, what I was saying to them was, "Do as I say and not as I do." What I desperately wanted to be able to say was, "Follow me as I follow Christ," but how could I say that when I wasn't following Christ and instead following the loud whispers? I realized the influence my life could have had on my children—after all, children learn by example—but I didn't know how to stop. I was a hypocrite, and I was stuck. "Help me, Jesus! I don't want this anymore. I don't want to live like this. It's too hard, and I'm tired of it."

Create in me a clean heart, O God; and renew a right spirit within me (Ps. 51:10).

One day, as I was praying, I heard the Lord say, *"Purge."* I got up, went through all of my hiding spots, and pulled out everything I had hidden. When I was done, I was surprised to see it all together. How much money had I wasted over the years? How much of my time had I given to evil? How much more of myself was I willing to give? NONE. I started breaking and ripping things up: movies (VHS and DVD), books, toys (yes, I had those too), and the erotic poetry I'd written. I did a second go-around and found more. By the time I was done, there was such a mess. I double-bagged it and threw it away. I felt so empowered. I had done it. As long as I was following the lead of the Father, I could do anything. It was all gone.

Then I realized I still had a problem.

"Okay, God, now what? I can't throw away what's in my head."

"Think on these things...."

"Finally, brethren, whatsoever things *are* true, whatsoever things are honest, whatsoever things *are* just, whatsoever things *are* pure, whatsoever things *are* lovely, whatsoever things *are* of good report; if *there be* any virtue, and if *there be* any praise, think on these things" (Phil. 4:8).

Was that it? Here I was thinking I'd get some long, complicated, hard-to-remember instructions. Could it really be as easy as "Think on these things"? I began to rebuke the thoughts and images that presented themselves and instead immediately thought about the freedom I felt and all the great things my God has done for me—and the things that were still to come. I thought about how He'd sacrificed Himself for my freedom and the love He has for me. I thought about how I was free to tell my children to follow me as I follow Christ. I thought about how He had made a way of escape for me. I thought about the grace and mercy He extended towards me. It really was that simple. I was able to resist the devil.

"Submit yourselves therefore to God. Resist the devil, and he will flee from you" (James 4:7).

The enemy still tries to bring those thoughts and images to my mind, but I know how to fight back now, and God continuously strengthens me to do so. I will continue to *"think on these things."* I will stay in His Word, spend time in prayer and meditation with Him, sing praises to Him, sing praises to Him, and sing praises to Him. I know I can never repay Him for all He has done and continues to do for me and my family, but I will keep praising and thanking Him for being **"my refuge and strength, my very present help in trouble" (Ps. 46:1).** Thank you Jesus.

Create in me a clean heart, O God; and renew a right spirit within me (Ps. 51:10).

How did the addiction affect your relationship with your husband?

No temptation has overtaken you except what is common to mankind. And God is faithful; He will not let you be tempted beyond what you can bear. But when you are tempted, He will also provide a way out so that you can endure it (1 Cor. 10:13).

This is the hardest part for me to talk about. I betrayed my husband for years because I was too ashamed to be completely honest with him. I believed the spirit of doubt when it told me that he would leave me if I ever told him. So, as usual, I kept my mouth shut. Before we got married, we talked about everything. We would talk for hours, but when he asked if I had ever watched pornography, I simply said yes and nothing more. Maybe it was something in my face or voice that stopped him from pressing the issue any further. Maybe he could hear the shame and guilt in my voice. Maybe he didn't want to know. Whatever it was, he didn't push for more information, and I was fine with that. That's when the betrayal and the communication block started. Instead of fearing the consequences, I should have given him the opportunity to help me, to pray with me and for me. But, I allowed doubt and fear to enter and change our relationship.

I was never physically unfaithful, but there was a constant battle going on in my mind, and that's where I was unfaithful. One of the dangers of pornography is that you don't need anyone else physically present to entertain you. The entertainment happens in your mind, and it could happen at any given moment. I could be sitting in a meeting, appearing to be paying attention, but totally caught up in something I had watched that was playing in my head. I fought continuously to keep my thoughts pure. Whenever my husband and I had a disagreement, instead of talking to him, I turned to my "friends." In the beginning of our marriage, we had an old VHS player that we'd bought at a flea market. It made a ridiculous amount of noise as it sucked in the tapes. It makes me laugh to think about that old thing now. Trying to sneak a movie was difficult back then because of that old noisy player. But then the world went digital and mobile. I went from trying to sneak a tape in the player to using my mobile device to download everything I needed while lying in bed next to my sleeping husband. I hated who I was as a married woman. How could I betray him in the way I was? He has since told me that sometimes he would awaken and catch me watching porn, but he didn't say anything.

There were several years during which I honestly didn't think my husband and I would still be married today. He stepped outside of our marriage, and I hated him because of it (that story is for another book and another time). Because of his infidelity, he felt he deserved to be cheated on, even if it wasn't physical, so he said nothing. He thought his actions caused me to watch pornography, so he said nothing (remember, at that point I hadn't yet told him that I'd hidden this addiction since I was nine years old). He said it bothered him greatly, but at the same time he was okay with it. Let me try to explain this. My husband said he was upset with me because he saw me go from watching porn just occasionally to watching it every other night, but at that point in our marriage, he didn't feel he had the right to question anything I did. He was angry with himself because he thought he had somehow opened that door for me. He was also upset with himself because he knew that his actions had caused me great pain and anger and had, therefore, caused me to turn from him and to pornography. So, by silently watching what I was doing, he could make the guilt that tortured him a little more bearable. Because he thought I was watching pornography and fantasizing about random men I'd encountered (I did tell him that because I wanted him to hurt) just to get even with him, it somehow made him feel better. So he silently continued to watch the addiction progress because in his mind, it made both of us feel better.

We were both in such terrible states then.

I was hurt and angry and disappointed. How could he do that to me? What had I done wrong? Was I not enough for him? I felt absolutely worthless. Not only could I not break away from my addiction, but I couldn't even make my husband happy. I had the worst breakdown I'd had. As usual, I turned to my medicine, but this time I didn't just watch—I replaced the female with myself. I wanted revenge, but I knew I could never bring myself to physically commit adultery, so I did what I thought was the next best thing. I chose random guys off the street and created totally new fantasies. In my mind, I fantasized about these guys and myself, everywhere I thought would hurt my husband: in his car, on his piano stand, on his motorcycle, in our home, in our marriage bed. I imagined him walking into our bedroom and catching me in the act, and I mused that I would laugh in his face. Even in our most intimate moments, when the whisperers told me that I wasn't satisfying my husband and that he was thinking about *her*, I would pretend I was with one of my guys. I was hurting, and I desperately needed and wanted him to feel what I felt. He didn't feel any of what I was doing to him because he wasn't aware that it was happening. I was only hurting myself. When I got caught up thinking about his infidelity and didn't want him to touch me, I used porn for satisfaction. It went on this way for several years.

It was extremely difficult to keep my focus on God during this time. I couldn't and didn't want to read His Word. I didn't want to sing anymore, but I did out of obligation. I was too ashamed to even call His name, and

Create in me a clean heart, O God; and renew a right spirit within me (Ps. 51:10).

certainly didn't try to enter His holy presence. Why would He want someone like me anyway? I was too vile a person to even think about entering the presence of God. I didn't want anything to do with anyone. If the people around me knew who I really was, they wouldn't have wanted me close to them either. In my mind, everyone knew about the affair, and they were laughing behind my back and calling me a fool for staying with him. I hated everyone. I just wanted to be left alone with my "friends."

I didn't think I would make it through this trial. I didn't know if I really wanted to. Another, more retched spirit was trying to slither its way in. I quickly shut it out, though. I might have been going to hell because of pornography, but I refused to go because of suicide. The battleground that my mind had become was soggy from the tears that poured from me. Trying to be normal and keep my secret was exhausting. Late one night, as I lay awake crying, I asked God why, on top of everything else I was dealing with, I had to deal with this also. From the depths of the darkness I heard, *"Now you can use your story to help others."* What did He mean? How could I help anyone in the condition I was in? I didn't want to help anyone. I didn't want to talk to anyone. All I wanted to do was leave my husband and everyone else and go so far away that I would never have to look into their faces again. I had made up my mind to do just that, but God wouldn't allow me. He sent someone to tell me not to leave my husband. He wanted me to know that my husband was a real Man of God who had made a mistake, and that He had big plans for the two of us and our children. The last thing I wanted to hear was that my husband was a Man of God. Such a hypocrite I was.

I was listening to a minister one day as he expounded on Proverbs 23:7. All of a sudden, the harsh reality set in: I was an adulterer as well. I knew that all the fantasies I played in my mind were wrong, but until that day, I'd never thought of myself as an adulterer. Everything I did happened in my mind only. I know some of you are questioning whether I truly betrayed my husband when I physically did nothing wrong. In my mind (heart), I did what I couldn't bring myself to do physically. So, was I really innocent? Proverbs 23:7 says **"For as he thinketh in his heart, so is he."** In my heart, I was committing adultery. I started thinking about how much I had betrayed my husband over the years, and it made me sick. What he had confessed to me was nothing compared to what I had done in my mind. I desperately needed my "friends" to comfort me, but now I couldn't even enjoy them because the whispering and laughing were louder than ever before: *"You're an addict and an adulterer."* The years of torment were starting to catch up with me, and I began to crash. I couldn't take anymore. The reality of it all was too much. I started to sink deep within myself, trying to find some relief, but I found none. I needed help, and I needed it quickly.

I was at the lowest point in my life and finally desperate enough to talk to someone without caring about the consequences. I couldn't go on the way I was.

Create in me a clean heart, O God; and renew a right spirit within me (Ps. 51:10).

I couldn't pretend anymore. I was tired, weak, and losing my mind.

The first step in the healing process is acknowledging that you have a problem. I'd never denied that I had a problem to myself, but what I needed was to OPEN MY MOUTH and confess the truth: that I had a problem and needed help. I talked to my First Lady-my pastor's wife (at that time) and let her know what I was dealing with and how I was feeling. We talked and she prayed.

(The whispering that was once so bold and confident had changed. Now I heard, *"No, no. Don't tell her. She can't help you!"* I couldn't believe it. They actually sounded afraid. The spirits were scared that I would tell the truth and gain my freedom. The power of truth had been within me the whole time. It all seems so simple now. Confess your sins, repent, and move on.)

She told me that when it happened again (she didn't say if; you can't say *if* it happens again to an addict because it *will* happen again), I should say aloud, "I am righteous because Christ is righteous." I did it, and such an awful feeling came over me. Not only did I become more disgusted with myself than ever before, it became clear to me that I was hurting God even more than my husband or myself. The more I pictured my Heavenly Father weeping for me, the less the breakdowns came. The more I concentrated on my God and the love He has for me, the less the fantasies played out in my mind. The more I prayed, read His Word, and surrendered myself to Him, the more I wanted to. A breakdown would still happen periodically if I wasn't in tune with the Lord. After all, it had been my nature since I was a young girl to handle problems and be satisfied in this way, and that didn't change overnight. However, now instead of carrying around the guilt of my actions and allowing that shame to stop me from appealing to my Father, I knew I could cry out to Him in repentance. I would remember the image of Him weeping for me and immediately repent for not leaning and depending on Him for help. If I had just talked to someone years ago, I wouldn't have had to deal with the guilt I carried for years. I could have dropped that baggage long ago.

Matthew 17:21 says **"Howbeit this kind goeth not out but by prayer and fasting."** I began to fast and pray like never before, and soon the weight started to lift. I felt light, and I allowed myself to rest in the presence and peace of God. He was transforming my mind. To be in His presence meant I had to stop thinking of pornography as my medicine and my comfort. Instead, I had to acknowledge it as the filth that I'd allowed to overshadow God for years. I allowed Him to wash my mind and change my thoughts. I let go of the years of shame and allowed Him to cleanse my mind and my soul.

"Purge me with hyssop, and I shall be clean: wash me, and I shall be whiter than snow" (Ps. 51:7).

He gave me beauty for ashes.

Create in me a clean heart, O God; and renew a right spirit within me (Ps. 51:10).

To appoint unto them that mourn in Zion, to give unto them beauty for ashes, the oil of joy for mourning, the garment of praise for the spirit of heaviness; that they might be called trees of righteousness, the planting of the LORD, that he might be glorified (Isa. 61:3).

Now, at moments when I'm least expecting it, my spirit will cry out, **"Create in me a clean heart, O God; and renew a right spirit within me" (Ps. 51:10)**. The words literally come out of my mouth. I give all praise, honor, and glory to my Lord and Savior Jesus Christ. He never gave up on me or my marriage. Restoration did come for my husband and me, but as I mentioned before, that story is for another book and another time. I love Christ because He first loved me.

How could you call yourself a Christian while addicted to porn?

For I do not do the good I want to do, but the evil I do not want to do–this I keep on doing. Now if I do what I do not want to do, it is no longer I who do it, but it is sin living in me that does it. So I find this law at work: Although I want to do good, evil is right there with me. For in my inner being I delight in God's law; but I see another law at work in me, waging war against the law of my mind and making me a prisoner of the law of sin at work within me. What a wretched man I am! Who will rescue me from this body that is subject to death? (Rom. 7:19-24).

"If you're not willing to stop sinning, how can you even call yourself a Christian?" I've asked myself this question for years. It's not that I wasn't willing to stop; I just didn't think I could. I had been living that way since I was nine years old. The problem was so much bigger than me. I wanted with everything in me to be free of the continuous battle raging in my mind, but it was there, and I couldn't deny it. The lust was there, the insecurities were there, the fear was there, and the self-loathing was there.

They had been with me since I laid my eyes on that first erotic article.

I was saved when I was twenty-four years old. It was during a time when I wasn't in a crisis or breaking down; I was able to completely open up and allow God to fill me with His sweet Holy Spirit. I heard no whispering from evil spirits. I could picture them cowering in the presence of this new Spirit I had allowed in. For a while, I was on fire for the Lord. I was studying His Word, praying and meditating, and growing more and more through the things of the Lord. It had been almost a year since I'd heard any whispering. Then I started to settle into my career. I got married, got busy with life. I started spending less time in God's presence and more time with the concerns of this world. I had stopped investing time into building a relationship with God.

I was sitting at my kitchen table grading papers one night when it happened. At first it was so faint that I couldn't make it out. I went back to my papers, and there it was again, louder this time. Immediately I knew what it was. Still I went back to my papers, and there it was again, in full force this time: *"You know you want it. It's been a long time. It will make you feel good. We don't have to say a word. No one will ever know."* Instead of going into my prayer closet, I focused on the fact that grades were due. I tried to ignore the voice, but it got louder. I sat there for another hour, finished my work, and went to bed. I was drained. Still, I hadn't prayed.

Create in me a clean heart, O God; and renew a right spirit within me (Ps. 51:10).

As soon as the teacher in me had finished her work the next day and headed home, there it was; it had been waiting for me. *"You know you want it. It's been a long time. It will make you feel good. We don't have to say a word. No one will ever know."* I didn't call on Jesus for help. I didn't really think about Him at all. I used my "free will" and began to justify what was about to happen. "Just one won't hurt. I'm filled with the Holy Spirit now, and I know He won't let me go too far. I can handle it now." Big, bad me. As soon as I opened the door that had been shut for almost a year, I didn't peek through "just for a little bit" as I'd intended. I stepped completely through the door, all the while pretending not to feel God's gentle pull. I was right about one thing: the Holy Spirit did make His presence known and tried to pull me back, but at that point I felt a stronger pull from something I was far more familiar with, something that was so wrong, but so right at the same time. The fisherman was back, with a stronger line this time. He had come back to claim the big one that had broken his line and gotten away. He succeeded. I almost pulled an all-nighter.

The next morning I awoke and heard nothing from any spirit. I felt defeated. How could I do this to God? I didn't pray that day because I was sure God didn't want to hear from me. I was sure He was angry that I'd ignored His gentle pull. I was sure that He had turned His face from me, had handed me over to the devil, and had left me for good. That surety caused me to fall so deep into the pit of pornography that I couldn't imagine anything or anyone able to reach me. Yet I was still able to help people who came to me, seeking advice. I still prayed for anyone who needed it. I still sang praises to God. It was as if falling into that pit had caused me to split into two people: one who enjoyed the things of the Lord and the warmth of His presence, and one who was terribly frightened of His wrath, but continued in sin, driven by the power of the loud whispers.

But, by some strange miracle, I soon felt that gentle pull again. I couldn't believe it at first. God had reached into the darkness and had begun to pull. He still wanted me! He still loved me! I wasn't a lost cause! That, however, was when the war really began to rage. I felt God's pull, but I still tried to hold on to her (the other me). Evil pulled her in one direction, and God pulled me in another. For so long the two parts of me had been indissoluble, and now we were being separated. All the pulling, pulling, pulling was making me sick. I knew I had to make a decision. I knew that if I wanted to continue in the things of God, I had to let her go. I chose Him because I wanted to always experience the feeling I got when I did what made Him happy. I liked making Him happy. I liked the image I had formed in my mind of Him smiling at me and saying, *"That's my girl."* My proud Papa. So, I chose Him. Just like that.

I felt her hand slipping from mine. I couldn't hold on anymore. I was too weak. She fell back into the pit's darkness, and I could hear her screaming for me to join her. She couldn't survive the darkness without me. But I couldn't. I didn't want the darkness anymore. I wept for her, for the adventures that had started when I was just nine years old. She was me, and she was gone. I had lost a piece of me, but I felt light and good. Wait…had she been the weight I'd felt all these years? She couldn't have been–she was my friend. Oh my goodness! She *was* the heaviness that had always been present with me. How could I not have known? I couldn't stop crying. All the years of thinking that something was holding me down, and all the time, it had been me. I'd been the one holding on to her. All I'd had to do was let her go. I couldn't stop crying. I cried for my lost time, my lost money, my lost years; I cried for my loss. After a while I "got over it" and moved on. Only this time, there were no zombies.

I did think about her every now and then, and if I got busy with the world and took my focus off of God, I would see if I could still hear her calling for me. However, every time I came close to the pit, I would feel God's gentle pull, would remember the darkness and the heaviness, and would gladly turn back. I was grateful for the freedom I felt. I had longed for it for so long, and I wasn't going to let anything take it from me.

I haven't gone back for a while now, and I don't want to. I live in the light now, and that's where I want to stay. I keep my light shining brightly so others can find their way out of the darkness.

Create in me a clean heart, O God; and renew a right spirit within me (Ps. 51:10).

It can happen to anyone. It may not be pornography that plagues you. It could be anything pulling you away from God's light and into the darkness of sin.

"Watch and pray so that you will not fall into temptation. The spirit is willing, but the flesh is weak" (Matt. 26:41).

"Wherefore let him that thinketh he standeth take heed lest he fall. Sin is sin and we all fall short of God's Glory" (1 Cor. 10:12).

We don't have to stay in that fallen state. Once we recognize that only God can provide the everlasting satisfaction we all seek, we can repent, accept His forgiveness, and get back up again. Make the decision to follow Christ today.

"And if it seem evil unto you to serve the LORD, choose you this day whom ye will serve; but as for me and my house, we will serve the LORD" (Josh. 24:15).

Freedom has been a long time coming, but thank God it's here. It was there all the time. It wasn't until I reached desperation that I was willing to do what was necessary to receive what was always mine. I had to stop believing the lies I had told myself for years: I need it to feel better, I can handle it, no one will ever know, it's not

Create in me a clean heart, O God; and renew a right spirit within me (Ps. 51:10).

affecting me. I had to deal with reality and truth. I had to remove the blinders and see my life as it really was. I had to see how the addiction was not only affecting me, but others around me. Ultimately, I needed to see how I was hurting God and how I had allowed guilt and shame to keep me from being and doing everything He had called me to do.

I'm excited to be at a point in my life where I am no longer ashamed to use my experiences to help others find freedom. I'm ready, are you?

Create in me a clean heart, O God; and renew a right spirit within me (Ps. 51:10).

A Prayer for Cleansing

Psalms 51:1-17

[1] Have mercy upon me, O God, according to thy loving kindness: according unto the multitude of thy tender mercies blot out my transgressions.

[2] Wash me thoroughly from mine iniquity, and cleanse me from my sin.

[3] For I acknowledge my transgressions: and my sin is ever before me.

[4] Against thee, thee only, have I sinned, and done this evil in thy sight: that thou mightest be justified when thou speakest, and be clear when thou judgest.

[5] Behold, I was shapen in iniquity; and in sin did my mother conceive me.

[6] Behold, thou desirest truth in the inward parts: and in the hidden part thou shalt make me to know wisdom.

[7] Purge me with hyssop, and I shall be clean: wash me, and I shall be whiter than snow.

[8] Make me to hear joy and gladness; that the bones which thou hast broken may rejoice.

[9] Hide thy face from my sins, and blot out all mine iniquities.

[10] Create in me a clean heart, O God; and renew a right spirit within me.

[11] Cast me not away from thy presence; and take not thy holy spirit from me.

[12] Restore unto me the joy of thy salvation; and uphold me with thy free spirit.

[13] Then will I teach transgressors thy ways; and sinners shall be converted unto thee.

[14] Deliver me from bloodguiltiness, O God, thou God of my salvation: and my tongue shall sing aloud of thy righteousness.

[15] O Lord, open thou my lips; and my mouth shall shew forth thy praise.

Create in me a clean heart, O God; and renew a right spirit within me (Ps. 51:10).

[16] For thou desirest not sacrifice; else would I give it: thou delightest not in burnt offering.

[17] The sacrifices of God are a broken spirit: a broken and a contrite heart, O God, thou wilt not despise.

Create in me a clean heart, O God; and renew a right spirit within me (Ps. 51:10).

Section 2

The Work

So that's my story. My closet is empty. Now, please allow me to help you empty yours. Let's do some work. Here are a few tools from my toolbox to help you get started on your journey to freedom.

Let's Do Some Reflecting

Think about your addiction, and list everything it does for you (i.e., What makes it enjoyable and keeps it going?).

_____

_____

_____

_____

_____

_____

Think about your addiction, and list everything it does to you (i.e., What don't you like about it?). Be specific.

_____

_____

_____

_____

_____

_____

Of the two lists above, which has effects that last longer? Why do you think this is the case?

_____

_____

_____

_____

_____

_____

Identifying the Triggers

The most important thing you can do to resolve the problem is gather the courage and motivation needed to face your triggers. Identifying your addiction's triggers will make it easier for you to identify what changes need to be made in order to positively affect your life. Let's identify these triggers.

Read the following questions. If the answer to any of these questions is yes, elaborate with any details you can think to include. This will help you recognize patterns and situations that cause the negative behavior.

Does watching certain shows or movies on TV trigger the desire?

_____

_____

Does listening to certain kinds of music trigger the desire?

_____

_____

Does feeling stressed, angry, or sad trigger the desire?

_____

_____

Does negative, critical self-thought trigger the desire?

_____

_____

Does being around certain people trigger the desire? Some relationships can be harmful, and coming to terms with this will only help you to move forward.

_____

_____

Create in me a clean heart, O God; and renew a right spirit within me (Ps. 51:10).

Let's Confront the Past

Let's make room for the joy of the Lord. If your heart is filled with past hurts, how can you open up and allow Him to fill you with anything new?

Is there anything hurtful/harmful from your past that still haunts you and causes you to turn to the addiction?

_____

_____

Have you talked to anyone about it? Why/why not?

_____

_____

How is your past keeping you from moving forward?

_____

_____

How is not dealing with your past hurting you and those around you?

_____

_____

Create in me a clean heart, O God; and renew a right spirit within me (Ps. 51:10).

DHR (Discard, Help, Replace)

I have a collection of items that contribute to my addiction. These are the items I will get rid of:

_____

_____

_____

_____

_____

_____

My addiction is triggered when I visit certain places. I will no longer visit these places:

_____

_____

_____

_____

_____

_____

There are only certain people I can trust and to whom I can talk. These are the people I trust to help me during my recovery from pornography addiction:

_____

_____

_____

_____

_____

_____

Keeping in mind that one addiction can replace another, think about some healthy/Godly activities you can do instead of watching pornography like: reading the Bible, praying, and meditating on God's goodness. I will choose these healthy/Godly activities instead of pornography when I am tempted.

_____

_____

_____

_____

_____

Create in me a clean heart, O God; and renew a right spirit within me (Ps. 51:10).

Scripture Chart

I'm not sure who's responsible for the below chart, which I saw on Facebook. It has helped me tremendously. Through these scriptures, I was able to see that the thoughts I had of myself were not that same as what God thought of me. They helped transform my self-thought. I know they will do the same for you.

You Say	God Says	Scriptures
I can't figure it out.	I will direct your steps	Proverbs 3:5–6
I'm too tired.	I will give you rest.	Matthew 11:28–30
It's impossible.	All things are possible.	Luke 18:27
Nobody loves me.	I love you.	John 3:16
I can't forgive myself.	I forgive you.	Romans 8:1
It's not worth it.	It will be worth it.	Romans 8:28
I'm not smart enough.	I will give you wisdom.	1 Corinthians 1:30
I'm not able.	I am able.	2 Corinthians 9:8
I can't go on.	My grace is sufficient.	2 Corinthians 12:9
I can't do it.	You can do all things.	Philippians 4:13
I can't manage.	I will supply your needs.	Philippians 4:19
I'm afraid.	I have not given you fear.	2 Timothy 1:7
I feel alone.	I will never leave you.	Hebrews 13:5

About the Author

Veronica Smith is a jewelry designer, owner of Celebrations by Veronica, and co-owner of Head 2 Toe Boutique. She has a background in secular education and served as a teacher and instructional coach for over 20 years. A certified Christian Life Coach and a member of the American Association of Christian Counselors, Veronica answered the call to ministry in 2008 and serves as minister and Sunday school teacher in her local church. Her goal is to spread God's word and help others gain freedom from the bondage of sin. Veronica lives in South Carolina with her husband and four children.

* 9 7 8 1 9 4 4 3 1 3 0 1 2 *